Table of Contents

Chapter 1: Introduction to AI Marketing

Understanding Artificial Intelligence Marketing

Artificial Intelligence (AI) marketing is a powerful tool that can help businesses of all sizes improve their marketing efforts. From predictive analytics to descriptive analytics, AI can provide valuable insights into customer behavior and preferences. By leveraging AI technology, businesses can create targeted advertising campaigns, optimize their communications and public relations strategies, and improve their content marketing efforts. In this subchapter, we will delve into the various ways in which AI can be used to enhance marketing across different niches.

Predictive analytics is a key component of AI marketing that can help businesses anticipate customer needs and behaviors. By analyzing historical data, AI algorithms can predict future trends and patterns, allowing businesses to tailor their marketing strategies accordingly. For small, medium, and large businesses, predictive analytics can provide valuable insights into customer preferences and help drive sales and revenue growth.

Descriptive analytics is another important aspect of AI marketing that can help businesses understand the current state of their marketing efforts. By analyzing data in real-time, businesses can gain a better understanding of their target audience and make more informed decisions about their marketing strategies. Whether it's improving advertising campaigns, optimizing content marketing efforts, or enhancing customer service, descriptive analytics can provide valuable insights that can help businesses achieve their marketing goals.

Advertising is one of the most common uses of AI in marketing, as businesses strive to create targeted and personalized ads that resonate with their target audience. By leveraging AI technology, businesses can analyze customer data to create more effective advertising campaigns that drive engagement and conversions. Whether it's through social media advertising, display ads, or email marketing, AI can help businesses reach their target audience more effectively and efficiently.

Communications and public relations (PR) are also areas where AI can make a significant impact. By analyzing customer feedback and sentiment, businesses can better understand how their brand is perceived and make adjustments to their messaging accordingly. AI can also help businesses identify influencers and thought leaders in their industry, allowing them to craft more targeted PR campaigns that resonate with their target audience.

In conclusion, AI marketing is a powerful tool that can help small, medium, and large businesses improve their marketing efforts across various niches. From predictive analytics to descriptive analytics, advertising, communications, and PR, AI technology can provide valuable insights that can help businesses drive sales, enhance customer service, and improve their overall marketing strategies. By understanding the various ways in which AI can be used in marketing, businesses can stay ahead of the competition and achieve their marketing goals more effectively.

Importance of AI in Marketing

In today's fast-paced digital world, the importance of artificial intelligence (AI) in marketing cannot be overstated. AI has revolutionized the way businesses reach and engage with their target audience, making marketing campaigns more efficient, personalized, and effective than ever before. From predictive analytics to customer service chatbots, AI technology is transforming the way businesses of all sizes connect with their customers.

One of the key benefits of AI in marketing is its ability to analyze vast amounts of data in real-time, allowing businesses to gain valuable insights into consumer behavior and preferences. By leveraging predictive analytics, businesses can anticipate customer needs and tailor their marketing strategies accordingly, leading to higher conversion rates and increased sales. This level of personalized marketing not only improves the customer experience but also helps businesses stay ahead of the competition.

In addition to predictive analytics, AI technology is also being used in advertising, communications, PR, content marketing, customer service, ecommerce, email marketing, sales, SEO, and social media. AI-powered chatbots, for example, can provide instant customer support and personalized recommendations, while AI algorithms can optimize ad campaigns for maximum ROI. By automating routine tasks and processes, AI frees up valuable time and resources for businesses to focus on strategic initiatives and creative endeavors.

For small, medium, and large businesses alike, incorporating AI into their marketing strategies is no longer a luxury but a necessity. In an increasingly competitive marketplace, businesses that fail to leverage AI technology risk falling behind their more innovative counterparts. By investing in AI tools and solutions, businesses can streamline their marketing efforts, improve customer engagement, and drive revenue growth.

In conclusion, the importance of AI in marketing cannot be ignored. From predictive analytics to social media advertising, AI technology is transforming the way businesses connect with their customers and drive results. By embracing AI as a key component of their marketing strategy, businesses can stay ahead of the curve and unlock new opportunities for growth and success in the digital age.

Overview of Predictive Analytics in Marketing

Predictive analytics is a powerful tool that has revolutionized the way businesses approach marketing. This subchapter will provide an overview of predictive analytics in marketing, exploring its uses, benefits, and best practices for implementation. By harnessing the power of data and machine learning algorithms, predictive analytics allows businesses to anticipate customer behavior, optimize marketing campaigns, and drive revenue growth.

One of the key uses of predictive analytics in marketing is customer segmentation. By analyzing customer data and behavior patterns, businesses can identify different customer segments and tailor their marketing strategies to meet the unique needs and preferences of each segment. This targeted approach allows businesses to deliver personalized messaging and offers that are more likely to resonate with customers, leading to higher conversion rates and increased customer loyalty.

Another important application of predictive analytics in marketing is lead scoring. By analyzing data on leads and prospects, businesses can assign a score to each lead based on their likelihood to convert. This allows businesses to prioritize their marketing efforts and focus on the leads that are most likely to result in a sale. By targeting high-quality leads, businesses can improve their conversion rates and maximize their return on investment.

In addition to customer segmentation and lead scoring, predictive analytics can also be used to optimize marketing campaigns. By analyzing past campaign performance and customer data, businesses can predict which marketing strategies are most likely to be effective in the future. This allows businesses to allocate their marketing budget more effectively, focusing on the channels and tactics that are most likely to drive results. By using predictive analytics to optimize their marketing campaigns, businesses can improve their ROI and drive revenue growth.

Overall, predictive analytics is a valuable tool for businesses of all sizes looking to improve their marketing efforts. By leveraging the power of data and machine learning algorithms, businesses can anticipate customer behavior, optimize marketing campaigns, and drive revenue growth. By understanding the uses, benefits, and best practices of predictive analytics in marketing, businesses can stay ahead of the competition and achieve their marketing goals.

Overview of Descriptive Analytics in Marketing

Descriptive analytics in marketing involves the use of data to understand past trends and patterns in order to make informed decisions about future marketing strategies. By analyzing historical data, marketers can gain valuable insights into consumer behavior, preferences, and trends, which can help them optimize their marketing campaigns and improve their overall performance.

One of the key benefits of descriptive analytics in marketing is the ability to track and measure the effectiveness of marketing campaigns. By analyzing data on key performance indicators such as website traffic, conversion rates, and customer engagement, marketers can identify which strategies are working and which ones are not, allowing them to make data-driven decisions to improve their marketing efforts.

Another advantage of descriptive analytics in marketing is the ability to segment customers based on their behavior and preferences. By analyzing data on customer demographics, purchase history, and interactions with the brand, marketers can create targeted marketing campaigns that are tailored to the specific needs and preferences of different customer segments, leading to higher conversion rates and increased customer satisfaction.

Descriptive analytics in marketing also plays a crucial role in identifying emerging trends and opportunities in the market. By analyzing data on industry trends, competitor performance, and consumer preferences, marketers can stay ahead of the curve and proactively adjust their marketing strategies to capitalize on new opportunities and stay competitive in the market.

Overall, descriptive analytics in marketing is a powerful tool that can help businesses of all sizes improve their marketing performance and achieve their business goals. By leveraging data to gain insights into consumer behavior, track campaign effectiveness, segment customers, and identify market trends, marketers can make smarter decisions that drive success in today's competitive business landscape.

Chapter 2: Implementing AI in Advertising

AI-Powered Advertising Platforms

AI-powered advertising platforms have revolutionized the way businesses reach their target audiences. These platforms utilize artificial intelligence to analyze data and optimize ad campaigns in real-time, ensuring maximum return on investment. For small, medium, and large businesses, AI-powered advertising platforms offer a competitive edge by providing advanced targeting capabilities and personalized messaging.

One of the key benefits of using AI-powered advertising platforms is the ability to target specific audiences with precision. These platforms use predictive analytics to identify potential customers based on their online behavior, demographics, and interests. By targeting the right audience, businesses can increase conversion rates and maximize their advertising budget. Additionally, AI-powered platforms can automatically adjust ad campaigns based on performance data, ensuring that ads are always optimized for maximum impact.

Another advantage of AI-powered advertising platforms is their ability to create personalized messaging for each individual user. By analyzing user data in real-time, these platforms can deliver targeted ads that resonate with each user on a personal level. This level of personalization not only improves the effectiveness of ad campaigns but also enhances the overall customer experience. For small, medium, and large businesses looking to build stronger relationships with their customers, AI-powered advertising platforms are a powerful tool.

In addition to targeting and personalization, AI-powered advertising platforms also offer advanced analytics capabilities. These platforms use descriptive analytics to track key performance metrics such as click-through rates, conversion rates, and return on investment. By analyzing this data, businesses can gain valuable insights into the effectiveness of their ad campaigns and make data-driven decisions to optimize their advertising strategy. For small, medium, and large businesses, this level of insight is invaluable in maximizing the ROI of their advertising efforts.

Overall, AI-powered advertising platforms are a game-changer for businesses looking to stay ahead in today's competitive market. By leveraging the power of artificial intelligence, businesses can target specific audiences, personalize messaging, and analyze performance data with unprecedented accuracy. For small, medium, and large businesses across all niches of marketing, AI-powered advertising platforms are a must-have tool for achieving success in the digital age.

Personalized Ads with AI

Personalized advertising has become a crucial aspect of marketing strategies for businesses of all sizes. By utilizing artificial intelligence (AI) technology, companies are able to create targeted ads that are tailored to individual consumers based on their preferences, behaviors, and demographics. This level of personalization has been shown to significantly increase engagement and conversion rates, making it a powerful tool in the digital marketing landscape.

One of the key benefits of using AI for personalized ads is the ability to analyze massive amounts of data in real-time. By leveraging predictive analytics, businesses can gain insights into consumer behavior and preferences, allowing them to create highly targeted ads that are more likely to resonate with their target audience. This level of precision not only increases the effectiveness of advertising campaigns but also helps to maximize return on investment.

In addition to predictive analytics, AI also enables businesses to utilize descriptive analytics to better understand the performance of their ads. By analyzing key metrics such as click-through rates, conversion rates, and engagement levels, companies can gain valuable insights into what is working well and what can be improved upon. This data-driven approach allows businesses to optimize their ad campaigns in real-time, ensuring that they are always delivering the most relevant and impactful messages to their target audience.

Furthermore, AI-powered personalized ads can also enhance customer service by providing a more personalized and seamless experience for consumers. By leveraging AI chatbots and virtual assistants, businesses can engage with customers in a more efficient and effective manner, providing personalized recommendations and support based on individual preferences and behaviors. This level of personalized interaction not only enhances the customer experience but also helps to build brand loyalty and trust.

Overall, personalized ads with AI have revolutionized the way businesses approach advertising and marketing. By leveraging predictive and descriptive analytics, companies can create highly targeted ads that resonate with consumers on a personal level. This level of personalization not only increases engagement and conversion rates but also enhances the overall customer experience. For small, medium, and large businesses looking to stay ahead in the competitive digital landscape, incorporating AI-powered personalized ads into their marketing strategies is essential for success.

Targeting Audience with AI

Targeting audience with AI is a crucial aspect of modern marketing strategies for businesses of all sizes. By leveraging the power of artificial intelligence, businesses can better understand their target audience's preferences, behaviors, and needs. This allows for more personalized and targeted marketing campaigns that are more likely to resonate with consumers and drive conversions.

One key way that AI can help businesses target their audience is through predictive analytics. By analyzing data from past campaigns, website interactions, and customer behavior, AI can predict future trends and behaviors. This enables businesses to anticipate what their audience wants and tailor their marketing efforts accordingly. Predictive analytics can help businesses identify potential customers, segment their audience, and create personalized marketing messages that are more likely to convert.

Descriptive analytics is another powerful tool that businesses can use to target their audience effectively. By analyzing data from various sources, such as social media, website interactions, and email campaigns, businesses can gain insights into their audience's demographics, preferences, and behaviors. This allows businesses to create targeted marketing campaigns that are more likely to resonate with their audience and drive engagement.

In addition to predictive and descriptive analytics, AI can also be used to target specific audiences through advertising. By utilizing AI-powered advertising platforms, businesses can create highly targeted ads that are shown to the most relevant audiences. This can help businesses reach their target audience more effectively and improve the ROI of their advertising campaigns.

Overall, targeting audience with AI is essential for businesses looking to stay competitive in today's digital landscape. By leveraging the power of artificial intelligence in predictive analytics, descriptive analytics, and advertising, businesses can better understand their audience and create more personalized and targeted marketing campaigns. This can help businesses drive engagement, increase conversions, and ultimately grow their bottom line.

Chapter 3: AI in Communications and PR

Chatbots for Customer Service

Chatbots have revolutionized the way businesses provide customer service in recent years. These AI-powered tools are designed to interact with customers in a conversational manner, providing them with quick and efficient answers to their queries. For small, medium, and large businesses, chatbots offer a cost-effective solution to handling customer inquiries and resolving issues in real-time.

One of the key benefits of using chatbots for customer service is that they are available 24/7, providing round-the-clock support to customers. This is particularly important for businesses that operate in multiple time zones or have customers located in different parts of the world. By leveraging chatbots, businesses can ensure that their customers always have someone to turn to when they need assistance, leading to increased customer satisfaction and loyalty.

In addition to being available around the clock, chatbots are also incredibly efficient at handling a high volume of customer inquiries simultaneously. Unlike human agents, chatbots can engage with multiple customers at once, reducing wait times and ensuring that no inquiry goes unanswered. This level of efficiency not only improves the overall customer experience but also allows businesses to streamline their customer service operations and reduce costs.

Furthermore, chatbots are capable of learning and adapting over time, making them increasingly effective at resolving customer issues. Through the use of machine learning algorithms, chatbots can analyze past interactions and make predictions about how to best respond to future inquiries. This predictive capability allows businesses to continuously improve the quality of their customer service and provide more personalized experiences to their customers.

Overall, chatbots are a valuable tool for small, medium, and large businesses looking to enhance their customer service operations. By leveraging AI technology, businesses can provide their customers with quick, efficient, and personalized support, leading to increased satisfaction and loyalty. As the use of chatbots continues to grow, businesses that embrace this technology will have a competitive advantage in today's fast-paced digital landscape.

AI-Powered PR Strategies

In today's digital age, the use of artificial intelligence in marketing has become increasingly prevalent. One area where AI can make a significant impact is in Public Relations (PR) strategies. By harnessing the power of AI, businesses of all sizes can enhance their PR efforts and achieve greater success. This subchapter will explore the various ways in which AI can be used to improve PR strategies and help businesses connect with their target audience more effectively.

One key way in which AI can revolutionize PR strategies is through the use of predictive analytics. By analyzing data from various sources, AI algorithms can predict trends and patterns in consumer behavior, allowing businesses to anticipate potential PR opportunities or challenges. This proactive approach can help businesses stay ahead of the curve and respond quickly to emerging PR issues.

Another important use of AI in PR strategies is in the realm of communications. AI-powered chatbots and virtual assistants can help businesses streamline their communication processes and provide faster, more personalized responses to customer inquiries. This can enhance the overall customer experience and build stronger relationships with consumers.

AI can also be utilized in content marketing to create more targeted and engaging PR campaigns. By analyzing data on consumer preferences and behaviors, AI algorithms can help businesses tailor their content to better resonate with their target audience. This can lead to higher engagement rates and increased brand awareness.

Furthermore, AI can assist businesses in monitoring and managing their online reputation. By tracking mentions of their brand across various online platforms, businesses can quickly identify and address any negative PR issues before they escalate. AI-powered sentiment analysis tools can also help businesses gauge public opinion and adjust their PR strategies accordingly.

Overall, AI-powered PR strategies have the potential to revolutionize the way businesses connect with their audience and manage their brand reputation. By leveraging the power of AI in predictive analytics, communications, content marketing, and online reputation management, businesses can enhance their PR efforts and achieve greater success in today's competitive market.

Using AI for Crisis Management

In today's fast-paced business world, crisis management is an essential skill for any organization. From natural disasters to PR scandals, businesses must be prepared to handle unexpected events that could potentially damage their reputation and bottom line. Fortunately, advancements in artificial intelligence (AI) have revolutionized the way companies can approach crisis management.

Using AI for crisis management involves leveraging predictive analytics to anticipate potential crises before they happen. By analyzing data from various sources, AI algorithms can identify patterns and trends that may indicate a looming crisis. This allows businesses to take proactive measures to mitigate risks and minimize the impact of a crisis on their operations.

In addition to predictive analytics, AI can also be used for descriptive analytics during a crisis. By analyzing real-time data from social media, news outlets, and other sources, AI can provide businesses with valuable insights into how a crisis is unfolding and how it is being perceived by the public. This information can help companies make informed decisions about how to respond to the crisis and communicate effectively with stakeholders.

AI can also play a crucial role in crisis communication and public relations. By using natural language processing algorithms, businesses can automate the process of monitoring social media and news outlets for mentions of their brand during a crisis. This allows companies to quickly identify and respond to negative sentiment, address customer concerns, and manage their reputation effectively.

Furthermore, AI can enhance crisis management efforts in other areas of marketing, such as advertising, customer service, and email marketing. By leveraging AI-powered tools, businesses can automate personalized communications with customers, tailor advertising campaigns to address crisis-related challenges, and provide timely and relevant support to customers during a crisis. Overall, integrating AI into crisis management strategies can help businesses navigate challenging situations more effectively and protect their brand reputation in the long run.

Chapter 4: Enhancing Content Marketing with AI

Content Creation with AI

In the world of marketing, content creation plays a crucial role in engaging customers and driving sales. With the advancements in technology, businesses can now leverage artificial intelligence (AI) to streamline and enhance their content creation process. In this subchapter, we will explore how AI can revolutionize content creation for small, medium, and large businesses across various niches.

One of the key benefits of using AI for content creation is its ability to analyze data and predict trends. By harnessing the power of predictive analytics, businesses can gain valuable insights into consumer behavior and preferences, allowing them to create more targeted and personalized content. This can help businesses stay ahead of the competition and drive higher engagement and conversion rates.

In addition to predictive analytics, AI also offers tools for descriptive analytics, which can help businesses understand the performance of their content and make data-driven decisions. By analyzing metrics such as engagement rates, click-through rates, and conversion rates, businesses can identify what is working well and what needs improvement, leading to more effective content strategies.

When it comes to advertising and communications, AI can help businesses create more impactful and persuasive content. By analyzing consumer data and behavior, AI can generate personalized ad copy and messaging that resonates with target audiences. This can lead to higher click-through rates, conversion rates, and overall ROI for advertising campaigns.

In the realm of content marketing and customer service, AI-powered tools can help businesses create and distribute content more efficiently. From generating blog posts and social media updates to responding to customer inquiries and feedback, AI can automate repetitive tasks and free up time for marketers to focus on strategy and creativity. This can result in more consistent and engaging content that drives customer loyalty and satisfaction.

Overall, AI has the potential to transform content creation for small, medium, and large businesses across various niches. By leveraging the power of AI for predictive and descriptive analytics, advertising, communications, content marketing, and customer service, businesses can create more targeted, personalized, and effective content that drives engagement, leads, and sales. With the right tools and strategies in place, businesses can stay ahead of the curve and achieve success in today's competitive marketing landscape.

Content Optimization with AI

Content optimization with AI is a crucial aspect of modern marketing strategies for businesses of all sizes. By utilizing artificial intelligence, businesses can streamline their content creation process, improve their search engine rankings, and enhance their overall digital marketing efforts. AI technology allows businesses to analyze data, predict trends, and make data-driven decisions to optimize their content for maximum impact.

One of the key benefits of using AI for content optimization is its ability to analyze large amounts of data quickly and accurately. AI-powered tools can review past content performance, identify patterns and trends, and provide insights on what type of content resonates with the target audience. This data-driven approach allows businesses to create more relevant and engaging content that is tailored to their audience's preferences, leading to higher engagement and conversion rates.

In addition to analyzing data, AI can also help businesses personalize their content to target specific audience segments more effectively. By leveraging predictive analytics, businesses can identify customer preferences, behaviors, and interests to deliver personalized content that is more likely to resonate with them. This level of personalization can significantly improve the effectiveness of content marketing campaigns and drive higher levels of engagement and conversions.

Another area where AI can significantly impact content optimization is in the realm of SEO. AI-powered tools can analyze keywords, trends, and search engine algorithms to help businesses create content that is optimized for search engines. By incorporating AI into their SEO strategy, businesses can improve their search engine rankings, increase website traffic, and reach a larger audience with their content.

Overall, content optimization with AI offers businesses a powerful tool to improve their digital marketing efforts across various channels. By leveraging AI technology, businesses can create more relevant and engaging content, personalize their messaging to target specific audience segments, and optimize their content for search engines. With the right AI-powered tools and strategies in place, businesses can enhance their content marketing efforts and drive better results in today's competitive digital landscape.

Content Distribution with AI

Content distribution is a crucial aspect of marketing that can greatly impact the success of a business. With the advancement of artificial intelligence (AI) technology, businesses now have the opportunity to optimize their content distribution strategies like never before. AI can revolutionize how businesses reach their target audience, increase engagement, and drive conversions. In this subchapter, we will explore how AI can enhance content distribution across various marketing channels for small, medium, and large businesses.

One of the key benefits of using AI for content distribution is its ability to analyze vast amounts of data to identify patterns and trends. With predictive analytics, businesses can anticipate consumer behavior and preferences to deliver personalized content to the right audience at the right time. This level of customization can significantly improve the effectiveness of content distribution, leading to higher engagement and conversion rates.

In addition to predictive analytics, AI also offers descriptive analytics that can provide valuable insights into the performance of content across different channels. By analyzing metrics such as click-through rates, bounce rates, and social shares, businesses can gain a better understanding of what content resonates with their audience and adjust their distribution strategy accordingly. This data-driven approach can help businesses optimize their content distribution efforts for maximum impact.

AI can also revolutionize content distribution in advertising, communications, PR, and other marketing channels. By leveraging AI-powered tools, businesses can automate the process of targeting, bidding, and optimizing ad campaigns to reach the right audience with the right message. AI can also help businesses streamline their communication efforts by analyzing customer feedback and sentiment to create more personalized and engaging content.

Furthermore, AI can enhance content distribution in ecommerce, email marketing, sales, SEO, and social media by automating repetitive tasks, such as scheduling posts, segmenting email lists, and optimizing product recommendations. By freeing up time and resources, businesses can focus on creating high-quality content that resonates with their target audience and drives results. Overall, AI can be a game-changer for businesses looking to stay ahead in the ever-evolving landscape of content distribution.

In conclusion, AI has the potential to revolutionize content distribution across various marketing channels for small, medium, and large businesses. By leveraging predictive and descriptive analytics, businesses can better understand their audience and optimize their content distribution strategies for maximum impact. With AI-powered tools, businesses can automate and streamline their content distribution efforts in advertising, communications, PR, ecommerce, email marketing, sales, SEO, and social media. By embracing AI technology, businesses can stay competitive, drive engagement, and achieve their marketing goals more effectively.

Chapter 5: AI Customer Service Solutions

AI-Powered Chat Support

AI-powered chat support is revolutionizing the way businesses interact with customers online. With the help of artificial intelligence, companies can provide instant and personalized customer support 24/7, improving customer satisfaction and loyalty. This technology uses predictive analytics to anticipate customer needs and provide relevant solutions in real-time, making it an invaluable tool for small, medium, and large businesses looking to enhance their customer service capabilities.

One of the key benefits of AI-powered chat support is its ability to handle a large volume of customer inquiries simultaneously. This means that businesses can provide instant responses to customers without the need for human intervention, saving time and resources. By automating routine customer service tasks, businesses can free up their employees to focus on more complex issues, improving overall efficiency and productivity.

In addition to handling customer inquiries, AI-powered chat support can also be used to personalize the customer experience. By analyzing customer data and behavior, businesses can tailor their responses to individual preferences and needs, creating a more engaging and personalized interaction. This level of customization can help businesses build stronger relationships with their customers and increase customer loyalty over time.

Furthermore, AI-powered chat support can also be integrated with other marketing channels, such as email marketing and social media, to create a seamless customer experience across multiple touchpoints. By leveraging AI technology to automate and personalize customer interactions, businesses can improve their overall marketing strategy and drive better results. This level of integration can help businesses optimize their marketing efforts and increase their ROI.

Overall, AI-powered chat support is a powerful tool for businesses looking to improve their customer service capabilities and enhance their marketing efforts. By leveraging the predictive analytics and personalized responses provided by AI technology, businesses can create a more engaging and efficient customer experience, leading to increased customer satisfaction and loyalty. For small, medium, and large businesses looking to stay ahead of the competition, AI-powered chat support is a must-have tool in their marketing arsenal.

Virtual Customer Assistants

Virtual Customer Assistants (VCAs) are becoming increasingly popular in the world of AI marketing. These intelligent chatbots are designed to provide personalized customer service and support to users, making them an invaluable tool for businesses of all sizes. VCAs are capable of understanding natural language and can engage in meaningful conversations with customers, helping to streamline the customer service process and improve overall customer satisfaction.

One of the key benefits of using VCAs in marketing is their ability to provide round-the-clock support to customers. Unlike human customer service representatives who have limited working hours, VCAs can be available 24/7, ensuring that customers can get the assistance they need at any time of the day or night. This can help businesses to improve their customer service response times and provide a more seamless experience for their customers.

In addition to providing support to customers, VCAs can also be used to gather valuable data and insights about customer preferences and behavior. By analyzing the conversations that customers have with VCAs, businesses can gain a better understanding of what their customers are looking for and tailor their marketing strategies accordingly. This can help businesses to create more personalized marketing campaigns that are more likely to resonate with their target audience.

VCAs can also be used to automate routine tasks such as answering frequently asked questions and processing orders. By taking care of these tasks, VCAs can free up human employees to focus on more complex and strategic aspects of their work, helping businesses to improve efficiency and productivity. This can ultimately lead to cost savings for businesses and a better overall customer experience.

Overall, Virtual Customer Assistants are a powerful tool for businesses looking to improve their customer service, gather valuable insights, and automate routine tasks. By leveraging the capabilities of VCAs, businesses can provide better support to their customers, improve their marketing strategies, and ultimately drive growth and success in today's competitive market.

AI for Customer Feedback Analysis

In today's digital age, customer feedback is more important than ever for businesses of all sizes. Understanding what customers are saying about your products or services is crucial for improving customer satisfaction and loyalty. Artificial Intelligence (AI) has emerged as a powerful tool for analyzing customer feedback in real-time and extracting valuable insights that can help businesses make informed decisions. In this subchapter, we will explore how AI can revolutionize customer feedback analysis for small, medium, and large businesses across various niches.

AI-powered predictive analytics can help businesses anticipate customer needs and preferences based on their feedback. By analyzing large volumes of customer data, AI algorithms can identify patterns and trends that can be used to predict future behavior. For example, AI can help businesses identify which products or services are likely to receive positive or negative feedback based on past customer interactions. This information can be invaluable for improving product quality, enhancing customer service, and tailoring marketing strategies to meet customer expectations.

Descriptive analytics, another key component of AI for customer feedback analysis, involves summarizing and visualizing customer feedback data to provide insights into customer sentiment and preferences. By leveraging natural language processing and sentiment analysis techniques, AI algorithms can categorize customer feedback into positive, negative, or neutral sentiments, and identify common themes or topics of discussion. This can help businesses identify areas for improvement, address customer concerns, and enhance overall customer satisfaction.

AI can also be used to optimize advertising and communications strategies based on customer feedback. By analyzing customer sentiment and preferences, AI algorithms can recommend personalized content, offers, and messaging that resonate with target audiences. This can help businesses increase customer engagement, drive conversions, and build brand loyalty. In addition, AI can help businesses track and analyze customer feedback across various channels, including social media, email marketing, and online reviews, to gain a comprehensive understanding of customer sentiment and preferences.

For businesses in the ecommerce industry, AI can revolutionize customer feedback analysis by providing real-time insights into customer behavior and preferences. By analyzing customer feedback data, AI algorithms can identify product recommendations, pricing strategies, and promotional offers that are most likely to resonate with customers. This can help businesses optimize their product offerings, improve customer satisfaction, and increase sales. Additionally, AI can help businesses automate customer service processes, such as responding to customer inquiries and resolving complaints, to provide a seamless and personalized customer experience.

In conclusion, AI has the potential to transform customer feedback analysis for small, medium, and large businesses across various niches. By leveraging AI-powered predictive analytics, descriptive analytics, advertising, communications, and ecommerce strategies, businesses can gain valuable insights into customer sentiment and preferences, optimize marketing strategies, and improve customer satisfaction and loyalty. As AI continues to evolve and become more accessible to businesses of all sizes, it is essential for professionals in the fields of artificial intelligence marketing to stay informed and embrace the opportunities that AI offers for customer feedback analysis.

Chapter 6: Optimizing Ecommerce with AI

AI-Powered Product Recommendations

In today's fast-paced digital world, businesses are constantly looking for ways to stay ahead of the competition and maximize their revenue. One of the most effective ways to achieve this is through AI-powered product recommendations. By leveraging the power of artificial intelligence, businesses can provide personalized product recommendations to their customers, leading to increased sales and higher customer satisfaction.

Predictive analytics plays a crucial role in AI-powered product recommendations. By analyzing customer data and behavior, businesses can predict which products are most likely to appeal to each individual customer. This allows businesses to tailor their product recommendations to each customer's unique preferences and needs, increasing the likelihood of a purchase.

Descriptive analytics is also essential in AI-powered product recommendations. By analyzing past customer interactions and purchase history, businesses can gain valuable insights into customer behavior and preferences. This data can then be used to create more accurate and targeted product recommendations, leading to higher conversion rates and increased customer loyalty.

Advertising is another key area where AI-powered product recommendations can make a significant impact. By using AI algorithms to analyze customer data and behavior, businesses can create highly targeted and personalized advertising campaigns. This not only increases the effectiveness of the advertising, but also enhances the overall customer experience by providing relevant product recommendations to users.

In conclusion, AI-powered product recommendations are a powerful tool for businesses looking to boost their sales and improve customer satisfaction. By leveraging predictive and descriptive analytics, businesses can create personalized product recommendations that cater to each customer's unique preferences. In addition, AI-powered product recommendations can also enhance advertising campaigns by providing targeted and relevant product recommendations to users. Overall, AI-powered product recommendations are a game-changer for businesses in the digital age.

AI for Inventory Management

AI technology has revolutionized the way businesses manage their inventory. From small startups to large corporations, AI has made inventory management more efficient and accurate than ever before. By using predictive analytics, businesses can forecast demand for their products and optimize their inventory levels accordingly. This helps reduce the risk of stockouts and overstocking, ultimately leading to cost savings and increased profitability.

One of the key benefits of AI for inventory management is its ability to analyze large amounts of data in real-time. By leveraging machine learning algorithms, businesses can quickly identify patterns and trends in their sales data, allowing them to make informed decisions about their inventory levels. This level of insight is crucial for businesses looking to stay competitive in today's fast-paced market.

In addition to predictive analytics, AI can also be used for descriptive analytics in inventory management. By analyzing historical sales data, businesses can gain a better understanding of their customers' buying behavior and preferences. This information can then be used to optimize product assortments and pricing strategies, ultimately leading to increased sales and customer satisfaction.

Beyond just managing inventory levels, AI can also be used to streamline the entire supply chain process. By automating tasks such as order processing, inventory tracking, and replenishment, businesses can reduce human error and improve overall efficiency. This not only leads to cost savings but also frees up valuable time for employees to focus on more strategic tasks.

In conclusion, AI has the potential to revolutionize the way businesses manage their inventory. By leveraging predictive and descriptive analytics, businesses can optimize their inventory levels, improve sales performance, and streamline their supply chain processes. Whether you're a small startup or a large corporation, incorporating AI into your inventory management strategy can help you stay ahead of the competition and drive business growth.

AI in Fraud Detection for Ecommerce

In the world of ecommerce, fraud is a constant threat that can have devastating effects on businesses of all sizes. This is where the power of artificial intelligence comes into play. By leveraging AI technology, businesses can significantly reduce their risk of falling victim to fraudulent activity. AI algorithms are capable of analyzing vast amounts of data in real-time to detect suspicious patterns and behavior that may indicate fraudulent activity. This allows businesses to take proactive measures to prevent fraud before it occurs.

One of the key benefits of using AI in fraud detection for ecommerce is its ability to adapt and evolve over time. As fraudsters become more sophisticated in their tactics, AI algorithms can continuously learn from new data and adjust their detection methods accordingly. This ensures that businesses are always one step ahead of potential threats, giving them a competitive edge in the fight against fraud. Additionally, AI can help businesses streamline their fraud detection processes, saving time and resources that can be allocated to other areas of the business.

Another advantage of using AI in fraud detection for ecommerce is its ability to provide real-time alerts and notifications. When suspicious activity is detected, AI algorithms can automatically trigger alerts to notify businesses of potential fraud. This allows businesses to take immediate action to investigate the issue and prevent any further damage. By detecting fraud in real-time, businesses can minimize the impact on their bottom line and maintain the trust of their customers.

Furthermore, AI can help businesses improve their overall security posture by identifying vulnerabilities in their ecommerce systems. AI algorithms can analyze data from multiple sources to identify potential weaknesses that could be exploited by fraudsters. By proactively addressing these vulnerabilities, businesses can strengthen their defenses against fraudulent activity and reduce the likelihood of falling victim to attacks. This proactive approach to security can help businesses build trust with their customers and protect their reputation in the marketplace.

In conclusion, AI has the potential to revolutionize fraud detection in ecommerce. By leveraging AI technology, businesses can proactively detect and prevent fraudulent activity, adapt to new threats, streamline their detection processes, provide real-time alerts, and improve their overall security posture. For small, medium, and large businesses looking to protect their ecommerce operations from fraud, investing in AI technology is a wise decision that can have a significant impact on their bottom line and reputation.

Chapter 7: Leveraging AI in Email Marketing

Personalization with AI

Personalization with AI is a powerful tool that businesses of all sizes can leverage to enhance their marketing strategies. By utilizing artificial intelligence, companies can tailor their marketing efforts to meet the specific needs and preferences of individual customers. This level of personalization can lead to increased customer satisfaction, loyalty, and ultimately, improved sales and revenue.

One of the key benefits of personalization with AI is the ability to analyze vast amounts of data to identify patterns and trends in consumer behavior. By understanding these patterns, businesses can create targeted marketing campaigns that resonate with their target audience on a more personal level. This can lead to higher conversion rates and a stronger connection with customers.

In addition to targeted marketing campaigns, personalization with AI can also be used to improve customer service. By utilizing chatbots and other AI-powered tools, businesses can provide personalized assistance to customers in real-time. This can help to streamline the customer service process, improve response times, and ultimately, enhance the overall customer experience.

Another important aspect of personalization with AI is its impact on ecommerce. By utilizing AI algorithms to recommend products to customers based on their browsing and purchase history, businesses can increase sales and drive customer engagement. This level of personalization can help to create a more seamless shopping experience for customers, leading to higher customer satisfaction and loyalty.

Overall, personalization with AI is a valuable tool for businesses looking to enhance their marketing strategies and improve customer engagement. By leveraging the power of artificial intelligence, businesses can create targeted marketing campaigns, improve customer service, and drive sales in a highly competitive market. With the right tools and strategies in place, businesses of all sizes can harness the power of AI to take their marketing efforts to the next level.

Automated Email Campaigns with AI

In today's fast-paced digital world, automated email campaigns with AI have become essential tools for businesses of all sizes. By harnessing the power of artificial intelligence, businesses can create personalized and targeted email campaigns that are more effective in reaching their target audience. This subchapter will explore the benefits of using AI in email marketing and provide practical tips for implementing automated email campaigns with AI.

One of the key advantages of using AI in email marketing is the ability to analyze large amounts of data to better understand customer behavior and preferences. By leveraging predictive analytics, businesses can anticipate the needs and interests of their customers and deliver more relevant and timely content. This can lead to higher engagement rates and increased conversions.

Another benefit of automated email campaigns with AI is the ability to create highly personalized and dynamic content. AI algorithms can analyze customer data in real-time to tailor email content based on individual preferences, behavior, and past interactions with the brand. This level of personalization can significantly improve the effectiveness of email campaigns and drive higher ROI.

Furthermore, AI can help businesses optimize their email campaigns by automating A/B testing and analyzing the results to identify the most effective strategies. By continuously testing and refining email campaigns, businesses can improve their overall marketing performance and increase their chances of success.

In conclusion, automated email campaigns with AI offer a wide range of benefits for businesses looking to improve their email marketing efforts. By leveraging the power of artificial intelligence, businesses can create more personalized and targeted email campaigns that drive higher engagement and conversions. With the right tools and strategies in place, businesses of all sizes can take their email marketing to the next level and achieve greater success in today's competitive marketplace.

AI for Email Analytics

AI for Email Analytics is a powerful tool that can revolutionize the way businesses analyze and optimize their email marketing campaigns. By leveraging artificial intelligence technology, businesses can gain valuable insights into their email performance, customer behavior, and overall campaign effectiveness. This subchapter will explore how AI can be used to enhance email analytics for small, medium, and large businesses across various niches such as predictive analytics, descriptive analytics, advertising, communications, PR, content marketing, customer service, ecommerce, sales, SEO, and social media.

One of the key benefits of using AI for email analytics is the ability to predict customer behavior and preferences. By analyzing large datasets of customer interactions, AI algorithms can identify patterns and trends that can help businesses anticipate what types of emails are likely to resonate with their audience. This predictive analytics can help businesses tailor their email content and timing to maximize engagement and conversions.

In addition to predictive analytics, AI can also be used for descriptive analytics to provide businesses with a deeper understanding of their email performance. By analyzing key metrics such as open rates, click-through rates, and conversion rates, businesses can gain valuable insights into which emails are driving the most engagement and revenue. This information can then be used to optimize future campaigns and improve overall email marketing effectiveness.

Furthermore, AI can also be used to enhance email advertising by leveraging machine learning algorithms to optimize email content and targeting. By analyzing customer data and behavior, AI can help businesses deliver more personalized and relevant email campaigns that are tailored to individual preferences and interests. This level of customization can help businesses improve their ROI and drive higher conversion rates from their email marketing efforts.

Overall, AI for email analytics offers a wide range of benefits for businesses looking to improve their email marketing performance. By leveraging the power of artificial intelligence technology, businesses can gain valuable insights into their email campaigns, predict customer behavior, optimize email content and targeting, and ultimately drive higher engagement and conversions. Whether you are a small, medium, or large business operating in any of the niches mentioned, incorporating AI into your email marketing strategy can help you stay ahead of the competition and achieve better results.

Chapter 8: Boosting Sales with AI

Predictive Lead Scoring

Predictive lead scoring is a powerful tool for businesses of all sizes looking to streamline their sales and marketing efforts. By using artificial intelligence and predictive analytics, businesses can accurately predict which leads are most likely to convert into customers, allowing them to focus their efforts on the most promising opportunities. This can lead to increased efficiency, higher conversion rates, and ultimately, more revenue for the business.

One of the key benefits of predictive lead scoring is its ability to save time and resources by prioritizing leads based on their likelihood of converting. By using data and algorithms to analyze lead behavior and characteristics, businesses can identify high-quality leads more quickly and effectively. This allows sales and marketing teams to focus their efforts on the leads that are most likely to result in a sale, rather than wasting time on leads that are unlikely to convert.

In addition to saving time and resources, predictive lead scoring can also improve the overall customer experience. By targeting the right leads with the right message at the right time, businesses can provide a more personalized and relevant experience for their potential customers. This can help to build trust and loyalty, ultimately leading to higher customer satisfaction and retention rates.

Another key advantage of predictive lead scoring is its ability to provide valuable insights and data that can be used to optimize marketing and sales strategies. By analyzing the patterns and trends in lead behavior, businesses can identify which marketing tactics are most effective at driving conversions, allowing them to refine their strategies for even better results in the future.

Overall, predictive lead scoring is a valuable tool for businesses looking to improve their sales and marketing efforts. By leveraging the power of artificial intelligence and predictive analytics, businesses can save time and resources, improve the customer experience, and optimize their marketing and sales strategies for maximum effectiveness. Whether you are a small, medium, or large business professional, incorporating predictive lead scoring into your marketing toolkit can help you achieve greater success in today's competitive business landscape.

AI-Powered Sales Forecasting

AI-powered sales forecasting has revolutionized the way businesses predict future sales trends and make informed decisions. By leveraging the power of artificial intelligence, businesses can analyze vast amounts of data to accurately forecast sales numbers, identify key trends, and make strategic decisions that drive growth and profitability. In this subchapter, we will explore the benefits of AI-powered sales forecasting and how businesses of all sizes can leverage this technology to gain a competitive edge in today's fast-paced market.

One of the key advantages of AI-powered sales forecasting is its ability to analyze historical sales data and identify patterns and trends that humans may overlook. By using advanced algorithms and machine learning techniques, AI can predict future sales with a high degree of accuracy, helping businesses make more informed decisions about inventory management, pricing strategies, and marketing campaigns. This not only saves time and resources but also enables businesses to stay ahead of the competition and adapt to changing market conditions.

Another benefit of AI-powered sales forecasting is its ability to provide real-time insights into customer behavior and preferences. By analyzing data from various sources, such as social media, website analytics, and customer reviews, AI can help businesses understand what drives customer purchases and tailor their sales strategies accordingly. This personalized approach not only improves customer satisfaction but also increases sales and revenue for businesses.

In addition to predicting sales trends, AI-powered sales forecasting can also help businesses optimize their sales processes and improve overall efficiency. By automating repetitive tasks, such as data entry, lead scoring, and forecasting, businesses can free up time for sales teams to focus on building relationships with customers and closing deals. This not only increases productivity but also leads to higher sales conversions and better overall performance.

Overall, AI-powered sales forecasting is a powerful tool that can help businesses of all sizes improve their sales performance, increase revenue, and gain a competitive edge in today's highly competitive market. By leveraging the latest advancements in artificial intelligence and machine learning, businesses can make more informed decisions, optimize their sales processes, and create personalized experiences for their customers. Whether you are a small, medium, or large business, AI-powered sales forecasting can help you achieve your sales goals and drive success in today's digital age.

AI in Sales Automation

AI in sales automation is revolutionizing the way businesses approach customer relationship management and lead generation. By harnessing the power of artificial intelligence, sales teams can automate repetitive tasks, analyze customer data to personalize interactions, and predict future sales trends with unprecedented accuracy. This subchapter will explore the various applications of AI in sales automation and provide practical insights for small, medium, and large businesses looking to leverage this technology to drive revenue and improve customer satisfaction.

One of the key benefits of AI in sales automation is its ability to streamline the lead qualification process. By analyzing data from various sources, AI-powered tools can identify high-quality leads and prioritize them for sales teams to follow up with. This not only saves time and resources but also increases the likelihood of closing deals with qualified prospects. Additionally, AI can help sales teams track customer behavior and engagement, enabling them to tailor their sales pitches and messaging to better meet the needs of potential customers.

In addition to lead qualification, AI in sales automation can also enhance the customer experience by providing personalized recommendations and targeted messaging. By analyzing customer data such as purchase history, browsing behavior, and social media interactions, AI can create tailored product recommendations and promotions that are more likely to resonate with individual customers. This level of personalization not only increases the likelihood of conversion but also fosters customer loyalty and satisfaction.

Another valuable application of AI in sales automation is its ability to predict sales trends and forecast future revenue. By analyzing historical sales data, market trends, and customer behavior, AI can generate accurate sales forecasts that help businesses make informed decisions about resource allocation, inventory management, and strategic planning. This predictive capability gives businesses a competitive edge by allowing them to anticipate market changes and adapt their sales strategies accordingly.

Ultimately, AI in sales automation is a powerful tool that can help businesses of all sizes improve efficiency, increase revenue, and enhance customer relationships. By leveraging the capabilities of artificial intelligence in lead qualification, customer personalization, and sales forecasting, businesses can drive growth and stay ahead of the competition in today's fast-paced digital marketplace. Whether you are a small startup or a large enterprise, integrating AI into your sales processes is a smart investment that will yield tangible results and position your business for long-term success.

Chapter 9: AI Strategies for SEO

SEO Keyword Analysis with AI

In the world of digital marketing, search engine optimization (SEO) is crucial for businesses to increase their online visibility and drive traffic to their websites. One key aspect of SEO is keyword analysis, which involves identifying the most relevant keywords that potential customers are using to search for products or services online. With the advent of artificial intelligence (AI) technology, businesses now have access to powerful tools that can automate and streamline the keyword analysis process.

AI-powered tools can analyze vast amounts of data to identify high-performing keywords that have the potential to drive organic traffic to a website. These tools use machine learning algorithms to predict which keywords are most likely to generate clicks and conversions based on historical search data. By leveraging AI for keyword analysis, businesses can gain valuable insights into their target audience's search behavior and tailor their SEO strategies accordingly.

One of the main benefits of using AI for keyword analysis is the ability to uncover long-tail keywords that are highly specific to a business's niche. Long-tail keywords are less competitive than broader keywords, making it easier for businesses to rank higher in search engine results pages. AI-powered tools can identify long-tail keywords that have high search volume and low competition, allowing businesses to target highly relevant keywords that are more likely to attract qualified leads.

Additionally, AI can help businesses identify semantic keywords that are related to their primary keywords. By incorporating semantic keywords into their content, businesses can improve their website's relevance and authority in the eyes of search engines. This can lead to higher rankings and increased organic traffic over time. AI can also analyze keyword trends and patterns to help businesses stay ahead of the competition and adapt their SEO strategies to changing search algorithms.

Overall, AI-powered keyword analysis tools can revolutionize the way businesses approach SEO and drive more targeted traffic to their websites. By leveraging the predictive analytics capabilities of AI, businesses can gain a competitive edge in the digital landscape and achieve sustainable growth through improved search engine rankings. For small, medium, and large business professionals, incorporating AI into their SEO strategies is essential for staying ahead of the curve and maximizing their online visibility and reach.

Content Optimization for SEO with AI

In today's digital age, search engine optimization (SEO) is crucial for businesses looking to improve their online visibility and attract more customers. With the help of artificial intelligence (AI), content optimization for SEO has become more efficient and effective than ever before. In this subchapter, we will explore the various ways in which AI can be used to enhance your content and improve your search engine rankings.

One of the key benefits of using AI for content optimization is its ability to analyze vast amounts of data in real-time. AI algorithms can quickly identify relevant keywords, analyze competitor content, and recommend changes to improve your own content's performance. By leveraging AI technology, businesses can ensure that their content is optimized for search engines and tailored to meet the needs of their target audience.

Furthermore, AI can help businesses stay ahead of the curve by predicting future trends and recommending strategies to capitalize on emerging opportunities. By analyzing consumer behavior and market trends, AI algorithms can help businesses create content that is not only optimized for SEO but also resonates with their target audience. This predictive analytics can give businesses a competitive edge in the ever-evolving digital landscape.

In addition to predictive analytics, AI can also be used for descriptive analytics to gain insights into how your content is performing. By analyzing metrics such as click-through rates, bounce rates, and time spent on page, businesses can identify areas for improvement and make data-driven decisions to optimize their content for SEO. This data-driven approach can help businesses track their progress, identify patterns, and make informed decisions to improve their overall SEO strategy.

Another way AI can enhance content optimization for SEO is through personalized recommendations. By analyzing user behavior and preferences, AI algorithms can recommend personalized content to users based on their interests and browsing history. This personalized approach can help businesses create more targeted content that resonates with their audience, leading to higher engagement and conversions. By leveraging AI technology, businesses can create a more personalized and engaging experience for their customers, ultimately improving their SEO performance and driving more traffic to their website.

Overall, content optimization for SEO with AI offers businesses a powerful tool to improve their online visibility, attract more customers, and stay ahead of the competition. By leveraging the capabilities of AI for predictive and descriptive analytics, personalized recommendations, and real-time data analysis, businesses can create content that is not only optimized for search engines but also resonates with their target audience. As AI continues to evolve, businesses that embrace this technology will have a competitive edge in the digital landscape and drive more traffic to their website.

AI for SEO Ranking Factors

In the ever-evolving world of digital marketing, staying ahead of the curve is essential for businesses of all sizes. One area that has seen significant advancements in recent years is the use of artificial intelligence (AI) for SEO ranking factors. By harnessing the power of AI, businesses can gain valuable insights into their website's performance and make data-driven decisions to improve their search engine rankings.

One of the key benefits of using AI for SEO ranking factors is the ability to analyze vast amounts of data quickly and accurately. AI algorithms can process information from a variety of sources, including website traffic, user behavior, and competitor analysis, to identify patterns and trends that can inform SEO strategies. By leveraging AI technology, businesses can gain a deeper understanding of how search engines rank websites and tailor their content and optimization efforts accordingly.

Another advantage of using AI for SEO ranking factors is the ability to predict future trends and changes in search engine algorithms. By analyzing historical data and using predictive analytics, businesses can stay ahead of the curve and adapt their SEO strategies to meet the evolving demands of search engines. This proactive approach can help businesses maintain their rankings and stay competitive in the ever-changing digital landscape.

In addition to predictive analytics, AI can also be used for descriptive analytics to provide businesses with a comprehensive overview of their SEO performance. By analyzing key metrics such as keyword rankings, organic traffic, and conversion rates, businesses can gain valuable insights into the effectiveness of their SEO efforts and identify areas for improvement. This data-driven approach can help businesses make informed decisions to optimize their website and improve their search engine rankings.

Overall, AI has the potential to revolutionize the way businesses approach SEO ranking factors. By leveraging the power of AI technology, businesses can gain valuable insights, predict future trends, and make data-driven decisions to improve their search engine rankings. Whether you are a small, medium, or large business professional, incorporating AI into your SEO strategy can help you stay ahead of the competition and drive meaningful results for your business.

Chapter 10: Harnessing AI in Social Media Marketing

Social Media Listening with AI

Social media listening is an essential tool for businesses of all sizes to understand their customers' preferences, sentiments, and behaviors. With the help of artificial intelligence (AI), businesses can now take their social media listening efforts to the next level. AI-powered tools can analyze vast amounts of data from social media platforms in real-time, providing valuable insights that can inform marketing strategies and decision-making processes.

One of the key benefits of using AI for social media listening is the ability to track and analyze conversations happening on various social media platforms simultaneously. AI algorithms can sift through massive amounts of data to identify trends, patterns, and sentiments that may be relevant to a business's marketing goals. By leveraging AI technology, businesses can gain a deeper understanding of their target audience's preferences and behaviors, allowing them to create more targeted and effective marketing campaigns.

In addition to tracking conversations, AI-powered social media listening tools can also monitor brand mentions, hashtags, and keywords relevant to a business's industry or products. This real-time monitoring enables businesses to stay ahead of trends, identify potential issues before they escalate, and capitalize on opportunities for engagement and promotion. By harnessing the power of AI for social media listening, businesses can proactively manage their online reputation and enhance their brand presence across various social media platforms.

Furthermore, AI can help businesses analyze the sentiment behind social media conversations, allowing them to gauge public perception and sentiment towards their brand, products, or services. By understanding the sentiment of online conversations, businesses can tailor their messaging and responses to better resonate with their audience and address any concerns or issues effectively. AI-powered sentiment analysis can also help businesses identify influencers and brand advocates who can help amplify their message and reach a wider audience.

Overall, social media listening with AI is a game-changer for businesses looking to enhance their marketing efforts and connect with their audience on a deeper level. By leveraging AI technology, businesses can gain valuable insights from social media data, track trends, monitor brand mentions, and analyze sentiment to inform their marketing strategies and decision-making processes. Whether you are a small, medium, or large business professional, incorporating AI into your social media listening efforts can provide you with a competitive edge in today's digital landscape.

AI-Powered Social Media Advertising

In today's fast-paced digital world, social media advertising has become a crucial component of any successful marketing strategy. With the rise of artificial intelligence (AI) technology, businesses now have the opportunity to leverage the power of AI to optimize their social media advertising efforts. AI-powered social media advertising offers a range of benefits, including increased efficiency, improved targeting capabilities, and enhanced ROI.

One of the key advantages of using AI for social media advertising is its ability to analyze vast amounts of data in real-time. By leveraging AI-powered predictive analytics, businesses can gain valuable insights into their target audience's behavior and preferences. This allows them to create highly targeted and personalized ads that are more likely to resonate with their audience, leading to higher conversion rates and increased ROI.

Additionally, AI-powered social media advertising can help businesses automate their advertising campaigns, saving time and resources. AI algorithms can continuously monitor and optimize ad performance, making adjustments in real-time to ensure maximum impact. This not only improves the efficiency of advertising campaigns but also frees up valuable resources that can be allocated to other important areas of the business.

Furthermore, AI technology can help businesses improve their social media advertising strategies by providing valuable insights into competitor activity and market trends. By analyzing data from various sources, AI algorithms can identify opportunities for growth and help businesses stay ahead of the competition. This enables businesses to make informed decisions about their advertising strategies and adapt quickly to changing market conditions.

Overall, AI-powered social media advertising offers businesses a powerful tool for optimizing their marketing efforts and driving success in today's competitive digital landscape. By leveraging AI technology to analyze data, automate campaigns, and gain valuable insights, businesses can take their social media advertising to the next level and achieve significant results. Whether you are a small, medium, or large business professional, incorporating AI into your social media advertising strategy is essential for staying ahead of the curve and reaching your target audience effectively.

AI for Influencer Marketing

In the world of marketing, influencer marketing has become a powerful tool for businesses of all sizes to reach their target audience and increase brand awareness. With the rise of social media platforms, influencers have the ability to reach millions of followers and have a significant impact on consumer behavior. As a result, many businesses are turning to influencer marketing as a way to boost their sales and grow their online presence.

AI technology has revolutionized the way businesses approach influencer marketing. By using AI algorithms, businesses can analyze data on social media platforms to identify the most relevant influencers for their target audience. This allows businesses to make more informed decisions when selecting influencers to partner with, ultimately increasing the effectiveness of their influencer marketing campaigns.

One of the key benefits of using AI for influencer marketing is the ability to predict the performance of influencer campaigns. AI algorithms can analyze historical data on influencer performance and audience engagement to predict how well a campaign will perform before it is even launched. This allows businesses to optimize their campaigns for maximum effectiveness and ROI.

Another advantage of using AI for influencer marketing is the ability to automate the process of identifying and partnering with influencers. AI algorithms can quickly analyze a vast amount of data to identify influencers who are the best fit for a business's target audience, saving businesses time and resources in the influencer selection process.

Overall, AI technology has the potential to revolutionize influencer marketing for businesses of all sizes. By leveraging AI algorithms to analyze data, predict campaign performance, and automate the influencer selection process, businesses can increase the effectiveness of their influencer marketing campaigns and achieve greater success in reaching their target audience.

Chapter 11: Conclusion and Future Trends in AI Marketing

Recap of AI Marketing Strategies

In this subchapter, we will provide a recap of the key AI marketing strategies that have been discussed throughout this book. These strategies are essential for small, medium, and large businesses looking to leverage artificial intelligence in their marketing efforts. By implementing these strategies, businesses can improve their marketing ROI, increase customer engagement, and drive revenue growth.

One of the key AI marketing strategies discussed in this book is predictive analytics. Predictive analytics uses machine learning algorithms to analyze historical data and predict future outcomes. By leveraging predictive analytics, businesses can anticipate customer behavior, identify trends, and make data-driven decisions to optimize marketing campaigns.

Another important AI marketing strategy is descriptive analytics. Descriptive analytics involves analyzing historical data to understand past performance and identify key patterns and trends. By using descriptive analytics, businesses can gain valuable insights into customer behavior, preferences, and purchasing patterns, which can inform marketing strategies and improve targeting.

AI can also be used to optimize advertising campaigns. By leveraging AI-powered algorithms, businesses can automate the process of creating, targeting, and optimizing ads to reach the right audience at the right time. AI can also be used to personalize ads based on individual preferences and behaviors, increasing the likelihood of conversion.

In addition to advertising, AI can also be used to improve communications and public relations efforts. By analyzing customer interactions and sentiment, businesses can use AI-powered tools to automate and personalize communication with customers, enhance brand reputation, and build stronger relationships with stakeholders.

Overall, AI can be a powerful tool for small, medium, and large businesses across various marketing niches, including content marketing, customer service, ecommerce, email marketing, sales, SEO, and social media. By implementing AI marketing strategies, businesses can drive growth, increase efficiency, and stay ahead of the competition in today's fast-paced digital landscape.

Emerging Trends in AI Marketing

In recent years, artificial intelligence (AI) has revolutionized the way businesses approach marketing. From predictive analytics to personalized advertising, AI has enabled companies to better understand their customers and create more targeted and effective marketing campaigns. As we look to the future, there are several emerging trends in AI marketing that are shaping the industry and providing new opportunities for small, medium, and large businesses to thrive.

One of the most prominent trends in AI marketing is the use of predictive analytics. By analyzing past customer behavior and trends, AI can help businesses predict future customer actions and preferences. This allows companies to tailor their marketing efforts to better meet the needs of their target audience and drive higher conversion rates. Predictive analytics also enables businesses to identify potential problems or opportunities before they arise, giving them a competitive edge in the market.

Another emerging trend in AI marketing is the use of descriptive analytics. This involves analyzing data to gain insights into customer behavior, preferences, and trends. By leveraging AI-powered tools, businesses can better understand their target audience and create more personalized and engaging marketing campaigns. Descriptive analytics also allows companies to track the success of their marketing efforts and make data-driven decisions to improve their overall strategy.

In addition to analytics, AI is also transforming the way businesses approach advertising and communications. AI-powered tools can analyze vast amounts of data to identify the most effective advertising channels and messaging for a specific audience. This allows companies to optimize their advertising spend and reach their target customers more efficiently. AI is also being used to automate customer communications, such as chatbots and virtual assistants, to provide real-time support and improve customer service.

Furthermore, AI is revolutionizing content marketing by helping businesses create more personalized and engaging content for their target audience. By analyzing customer data and preferences, AI can suggest topics, formats, and distribution channels that are likely to resonate with customers. This not only improves the effectiveness of content marketing efforts but also helps businesses build stronger relationships with their audience. AI is also being used to optimize email marketing campaigns, sales processes, and SEO strategies to drive more traffic and conversions.

Overall, the emerging trends in AI marketing are providing businesses with new opportunities to better understand their customers, create more targeted marketing campaigns, and drive higher ROI. By leveraging the power of AI, small, medium, and large businesses can stay ahead of the competition and achieve long-term success in today's dynamic market. It is essential for business professionals in all niches - from advertising to customer service to ecommerce - to embrace AI marketing and harness its potential to drive growth and innovation.

The Future of AI in Marketing

As we look ahead to the future of AI in marketing, it is clear that this technology will continue to revolutionize the way businesses engage with their customers. From predictive analytics to descriptive analytics, advertising to customer service, AI is already being used in a variety of ways to enhance marketing efforts across all industries. In the coming years, we can expect to see even more advancements in AI technology that will further streamline and optimize marketing processes for small, medium, and large businesses alike.

One of the key areas where AI is expected to make a significant impact in the future is in the realm of personalized marketing. By leveraging predictive analytics and machine learning algorithms, businesses will be able to analyze vast amounts of data to better understand the preferences and behaviors of individual customers. This will allow marketers to deliver more targeted and relevant content to their audience, leading to higher engagement and conversion rates.

Additionally, AI is poised to revolutionize the way businesses approach customer service. With the help of chatbots and virtual assistants powered by AI, companies can provide round-the-clock support to their customers, resolving issues and answering questions in real-time. This not only improves the overall customer experience but also helps businesses save time and resources by automating routine tasks.

In the realm of advertising and communications, AI will continue to play a crucial role in helping businesses optimize their marketing strategies. By analyzing consumer behavior and market trends, AI algorithms can help businesses identify the most effective channels and messages to reach their target audience. This level of precision and efficiency will not only improve the ROI of marketing campaigns but also enable businesses to stay ahead of the competition in an increasingly crowded marketplace.

In conclusion, the future of AI in marketing holds immense potential for businesses of all sizes and industries. By leveraging the power of AI technologies such as predictive analytics, descriptive analytics, and machine learning, businesses can unlock new opportunities to engage with customers, streamline marketing processes, and drive growth. As AI continues to evolve and become more sophisticated, it is essential for businesses to stay informed and adapt their marketing strategies accordingly to stay competitive in the ever-changing landscape of digital marketing.

Appendix: Resources for AI Marketing Professionals

In this subchapter, we have compiled a list of valuable resources for AI marketing professionals to enhance their skills and stay updated on the latest trends in the industry. Whether you are a small business owner looking to implement AI strategies in your marketing efforts or a large corporation seeking to optimize your existing AI tools, these resources will provide you with the knowledge and tools necessary to succeed in the competitive world of AI marketing.

One of the key resources for AI marketing professionals is the AI Marketing Institute, which offers online courses, webinars, and workshops on various aspects of AI marketing, including predictive analytics, advertising, and social media. The institute provides valuable insights and practical tips on how to leverage AI technologies to improve marketing ROI and drive business growth.

For those interested in staying up-to-date on the latest AI marketing trends and best practices, we recommend subscribing to industry-leading publications such as Adweek, Marketing Land, and AI Business. These publications regularly feature articles, case studies, and interviews with top AI marketing experts, providing valuable insights and inspiration for professionals looking to take their marketing strategies to the next level.

In addition to online resources, attending AI marketing conferences and networking events can be a great way to connect with industry professionals, exchange ideas, and stay current on the latest AI marketing trends. Some of the top AI marketing conferences include the AI Summit, Marketing Artificial Intelligence Conference (MAICON), and AI in Marketing Summit.

Lastly, for professionals looking to deepen their knowledge of AI marketing and gain hands-on experience with AI tools and technologies, we recommend exploring online platforms such as Coursera, Udemy, and LinkedIn Learning, which offer a wide range of courses on AI marketing, predictive analytics, and other relevant topics. By investing in continued learning and professional development, AI marketing professionals can stay ahead of the curve and drive success for their businesses in today's increasingly competitive marketplace.

100 AI Marketing Companies

1. **Pecan AI** - Predictive analytics and data preparation.
2. **Oolo AI** - Customer service solutions and revenue optimization.
3. **Appier** - AI-driven marketing and cross-screen targeting.
4. **aix** - Digital marketing solutions in Japan and globally.
5. **SmartSites** - SEO, content generation, and personalized marketing.
6. **Influencity** - Influencer marketing and audience quality scoring.
7. **Jasper.ai** - Content generation and language translation.
8. **Yotpo** - User-generated content and eCommerce retention marketing.
9. **Clickstrike** - General AI-driven marketing solutions.
10. **Avantgrade** - Digital marketing with a focus on AI.
11. **NoGood** - Growth marketing and AI optimization.
12. **SingleGrain** - SEO and PPC with AI.
13. **Matrix Marketing Group** - Customer segmentation and product marketing.
14. **Deep Cognition** - AI-powered automation for marketing processes.
15. **Albert** - Autonomous digital marketing campaigns.
16. **Acquisio** - AI for PPC campaign management.
17. **Pathmatics** - Advertising intelligence and analytics.
18. **Fractal Analytics** - AI-driven insights and analytics.
19. **Sprinklr** - Unified customer experience management with AI.
20. **Bluecore** - AI for retail marketing.
21. **Blueshift** - AI-powered customer engagement.
22. **Cortex** - AI-driven social media optimization.
23. **Crimson Hexagon** - Social media analytics and AI.
24. **Emarsys** - Omnichannel customer engagement with AI.
25. **GumGum** - Contextual advertising with AI.
26. **Hootsuite** - Social media management and analytics.
27. **Insider** - AI for customer experience personalization.
28. **Kenshoo** - AI for marketing optimization.
29. **Phrasee** - AI for email marketing and content generation.
30. **Quantcast** - AI-driven audience insights.
31. **Rev.ai** - Speech-to-text and audio intelligence.
32. **Sailthru** - AI for personalized marketing.
33. **Selligent** - Omnichannel marketing with AI.
34. **Sizmek** - AI for ad management and analytics.
35. **Tact.ai** - AI for sales and marketing automation.
36. **ThreatMetrix** - AI for fraud prevention in marketing.
37. **Thunder** - Creative management platform with AI.
38. **Unmetric** - AI for social media benchmarking.

39. **Vee24** - AI-powered customer engagement.
40. **Voysis** - AI for voice commerce.
41. **Zeta Global** - AI for customer lifecycle marketing.
42. **6sense** - AI-driven account-based marketing.
43. **Adverity** - Marketing data integration and AI analytics.
44. **Aible** - AI for predictive and prescriptive analytics.
45. **Amperity** - Customer data platform with AI.
46. **Bidalgo** - AI for app marketing.
47. **Brand24** - Social media monitoring and analytics.
48. **Chorus.ai** - Conversation analytics for sales teams.
49. **Conversica** - AI for sales and marketing conversations.
50. **Drift** - AI for conversational marketing.
51. **Funnel** - Data collection and analysis with AI.
52. **Invoca** - Call tracking and analytics with AI.
53. **Lattice Engines** - AI for account-based marketing.
54. **Leanplum** - Mobile marketing with AI.
55. **Lytics** - Customer data platform with AI.
56. **Madgicx** - AI for ad campaign optimization.
57. **Mapp Digital** - Customer experience platform with AI.
58. **Optimizely** - Experimentation and personalization with AI.
59. **Outbrain** - Content discovery platform with AI.
60. **Pardot** - B2B marketing automation with AI.
61. **Percolate** - Marketing orchestration with AI.
62. **SAS Customer Intelligence** - AI for marketing analytics.
63. **Sentient Technologies** - AI for ecommerce and marketing.
64. **Signal AI** - Media monitoring and analytics.
65. **Synthesio** - Social media intelligence with AI.
66. **TapClicks** - Marketing reporting and analytics with AI.
67. **Tealium** - Customer data platform with AI.
68. **TruSignal** - Predictive scoring with AI.
69. **Zalster** - AI for ad campaign automation.
70. **Zignal Labs** - Media intelligence and analytics.
71. **ZineOne** - Real-time personalization with AI.
72. **Zylotech** - Customer data platform with AI.
73. **Adobe Sensei** - AI and machine learning in digital media and marketing.
74. **IBM Watson Marketing** - AI for marketing analytics and customer insights.
75. **Microsoft Dynamics 365 AI** - AI for sales and marketing.
76. **Salesforce Einstein** - AI for CRM and marketing automation.
77. **Google AI** - AI tools for advertising and analytics.

78. **Facebook AI** - AI for social media marketing and advertising.
79. **Amazon AI** - AI for ecommerce and advertising.
80. **Alibaba DAMO Academy** - AI research and applications in marketing.
81. **Tencent AI Lab** - AI for social media and gaming marketing.
82. **Baidu Research** - AI for search and advertising.
83. **NVIDIA AI** - AI for graphics and visualization in marketing.
84. **Oracle AI** - AI for enterprise marketing solutions.
85. **SAP Leonardo** - AI for digital transformation in marketing.
86. **Cognitivescale** - AI for customer experience and engagement.
87. **DataRobot** - Automated machine learning for marketing analytics.
88. **H2O.ai** - Open-source AI for marketing analytics.
89. **SparkCognition** - AI for cybersecurity in marketing.
90. **Clarifai** - Computer vision AI for visual marketing.
91. **CloudMinds** - AI for robotics and automation in marketing.
92. **Element AI** - AI research and solutions for marketing.
93. **iFlytek** - AI for voice recognition in marketing.
94. **Preferred Networks** - AI for deep learning in marketing.
95. **SenseTime** - AI for computer vision and image recognition in marketing.
96. **Megvii** - AI for facial recognition in marketing.
97. **Yitu Technology** - AI for computer vision and medical imaging in marketing.
98. **CloudWalk** - AI for facial recognition and fintech marketing.
99. **Hikvision** - AI for surveillance and security marketing.
100. **Face++** - AI for facial recognition and smart retail marketing.

100 Top AI Marketing Software

- **Jasper.ai** - AI-driven content generation and art creation.
- **Copy.ai** - Automated copywriting for various content needs.
- **Canva** - AI-powered graphic design tool.
- **Midjourney** - AI for creating advanced graphics.
- **Synthesia** - AI avatars for video creation.
- **Murf.ai** - Realistic AI voice generation.
- **Flick** - AI for social media content creation.
- **Zapier** - No-code automation for various marketing tasks.
- **Influencity** - Influencer marketing and audience quality scoring.
- **Yotpo** - User-generated content and eCommerce retention.
- **LookaAI** - AI-powered logo and brand kit creation.
- **HubSpot** - AI for CRM and marketing automation.
- **Salesforce Einstein** - AI for customer relationship management.
- **Adobe Sensei** - AI for creative and marketing workflows.
- **Hootsuite** - Social media management with AI capabilities.
- **Buffer** - Social media scheduling and analytics with AI.
- **Sprout Social** - AI for social media engagement and analytics.
- **Lumen5** - AI video creation from text content.
- **AdCreative.ai** - Automated ad creative generation.
- **Seventh Sense** - AI for email marketing optimization.
- **Crimson Hexagon** - Social media analytics with AI.
- **Pathmatics** - Ad intelligence and analytics.
- **Sprinklr** - Unified customer experience management.
- **Blueshift** - AI for cross-channel marketing.
- **Kenshoo** - AI for marketing optimization.
- **Phrasee** - AI for email and marketing copywriting.
- **Smartly.io** - AI-powered social media ad management.
- **Albert** - Autonomous digital marketing campaigns.
- **Acquisio** - AI for PPC campaign management.
- **Brand24** - Media monitoring with AI.
- **Frase** - AI for content creation and optimization.
- **BrightEdge** - AI for SEO and content performance.
- **MarketMuse** - AI for content research and optimization.
- **Conversica** - AI for lead generation and sales.
- **Chorus.ai** - AI for conversation analytics.
- **Invoca** - Call tracking and analytics with AI.

- **Lattice Engines** - AI for account-based marketing.
- **Leanplum** - Mobile marketing with AI.
- **Lytics** - Customer data platform with AI.
- **Madgicx** - AI for ad campaign optimization.
- **Mapp Digital** - Customer experience platform.
- **Optimizely** - Experimentation and personalization with AI.
- **Outbrain** - Content discovery platform.
- **Pardot** - B2B marketing automation with AI.
- **Percolate** - Marketing orchestration with AI.
- **SAS Customer Intelligence** - Marketing analytics with AI.
- **Signal AI** - Media monitoring and analytics.
- **Synthesio** - Social media intelligence with AI.
- **TapClicks** - Marketing reporting and analytics.
- **Tealium** - Customer data platform with AI.
- **TruSignal** - Predictive scoring with AI.
- **Zalster** - AI for ad campaign automation.
- **Zignal Labs** - Media intelligence and analytics.
- **ZineOne** - Real-time personalization with AI.
- **Zylotech** - Customer data platform with AI.
- **Adobe Photoshop Lightroom** - AI-powered photo editing.
- **Descript** - AI for video and audio editing.
- **ClickUp** - Project management with AI features.
- **ActiveCampaign** - Customer experience automation with AI.
- **Mailchimp** - Email marketing with AI features.
- **Drift** - Conversational marketing and sales with AI.
- **Intercom** - Customer messaging platform with AI.
- **Pendo** - Product analytics and user guidance with AI.
- **Segment** - Customer data platform with AI.
- **HubSpot Marketing Hub** - Comprehensive marketing platform with AI.
- **Google Analytics** - Web analytics with AI insights.
- **Hotjar** - Website heatmaps and behavior analytics with AI.
- **Crazy Egg** - Visual website analytics with AI.
- **Heap Analytics** - Web analytics with AI.
- **FullStory** - Digital experience analytics with AI.
- **Kissmetrics** - Customer engagement analytics with AI.
- **Mixpanel** - Product analytics with AI.
- **Amplitude** - Product analytics with AI.

- **Looker** - Business intelligence with AI.
- **Tableau** - Data visualization with AI insights.
- **Microsoft Power BI** - Business intelligence with AI.
- **Qlik** - Data discovery and analytics with AI.
- **Sisense** - Business intelligence with AI.
- **Domo** - Business intelligence and data visualization with AI.
- **Google Data Studio** - Data visualization with AI.
- **Chartio** - Business intelligence with AI.
- **Mode Analytics** - Business intelligence with AI.
- **Alteryx** - Data analytics with AI.
- **RapidMiner** - Data science and machine learning platform.
- **KNIME** - Open-source data analytics with AI.
- **Databricks** - Data engineering and machine learning.
- **H2O.ai** - Open-source AI and machine learning.
- **DataRobot** - Automated machine learning platform.
- **SAS Viya** - AI and analytics platform.
- **IBM Watson Studio** - AI and data science platform.
- **Amazon SageMaker** - Machine learning platform.
- **Azure Machine Learning** - Machine learning platform.
- **Google AI Platform** - Machine learning platform.
- **BigML** - Machine learning platform.
- **MLflow** - Open-source platform for machine learning.
- **Keras** - Deep learning framework.
- **TensorFlow** - Open-source machine learning framework.
- **PyTorch** - Open-source machine learning framework.
- **Apache MXNet** - Deep learning framework.
- **Caffe** - Deep learning framework.

www.ingramcontent.com/pod-product-compliance
Lightning Source LLC
Chambersburg PA
CBHW082124220526
45472CB00009B/2292